Reducing the use of restrictive practices with people who have intellectual disabilities

A practical approach

David Allen

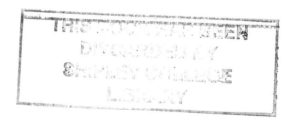

British Library Cataloguing in Publication Data
A CIP record for this book is available from the Public Library

© BILD Publications 2011

BILD Publications is the imprint of:
British Institute of Learning Disabilities
Campion House
Green Street
Kidderminster
Worcestershire DY10 1JL

Telephone: 01562 723010
Fax: 01562 723029
E-mail: enquiries@bild.org.uk
Website: www.bild.org.uk

ISBN 978 1 905218 23 3

BILD Publications are distributed by:
BookSource
50 Cambuslang Road
Cambuslang
Glasgow G32 8NB

Telephone: 0845 370 0067
Fax: 0845 370 0068

For a publications catalogue with details of all BILD books and journals telephone
01562 723010, e-mail enquiries@bild.org.uk or visit the BILD website www.bild.org.uk

Printed in the UK by Latimer Trend & Company Ltd, Plymouth

The British Institute of Learning Disabilities is committed to improving the quality of life
for people with a learning disability by involving them and their families in all aspects of
our work, working with government and public bodies to achieve full citizenship,
undertaking beneficial research and development projects and helping service
providers to develop and share good practice.

Contents

Acknowledgements

My thanks are due to Neil Kaye, Edwin Jones and Robin Gunson for their helpful comments on an earlier draft of this publication and to Lauren Carter and Laura Barrett for their assistance with the literature search.

1. Introduction

The use of restrictive practices (such as restraint, seclusion and as required medication) are unfortunately commonplace in services that support people with intellectual disabilities who present additional complex behavioural or mental health needs. Concerns about such interventions regularly surface in official investigations into the quality of care afforded to such individuals, in media exposés, in individual stories about service user experience and, to a lesser extent, in the research literature.

Since the mid-1990s, the British Institute of Learning Disabilities (BILD) has been engaged in a programme of work that has aimed to address many of these concerns. Recognising that reactive behaviour management interventions are sometimes an important, albeit minor, component of effective intervention plans for people with challenging behaviours, this initially focussed on improving and regulating how physical intervention training was delivered to carers in the UK (Harris et al, 1996; Jefferson, 2009). This was leading-edge work given that the prevailing form of training in UK services at that time posed significant ethical issues and that there was no existing form of accreditation for such training available. Later, guidance was provided on both the use of time-out and seclusion (Paley, 2009). In more recent years, the organisation's focus has changed and it has now more appropriately located its continuing interest in improving practice in physical intervention within an overall context of developing positive behavioural support (PBS) as a preferred intervention model.

BILD has therefore already done a great deal to improve how restrictive physical practices are trained and delivered in the UK. However, even though we can make significant improvements in how we restrain (notably by avoiding the use of deliberate pain and particularly high-risk restraint positions) and contain (by improving the traditionally barren nature of environments used for this purpose), the use of restrictive practices is likely to remain inherently aversive for those who experience them. Therefore, we must be able to ensure that their use is always minimal, ethical and justifiable. Unfortunately, rather than being a last resort, in many services they remain a first and only resort in the absence of carers being able to deliver effective therapeutic alternatives.

This book continues BILD's strategy to improve practice in this area by focussing on reducing the use of restrictive procedures in a structured and accessible way.

The content is laid out as follows. First, what we know about how often restrictive practices are used with people with intellectual disabilities and their potential impact is discussed; this is sobering reading and in itself provides justification for this publication. Next, lessons about the key individual and organisational factors that can lead to reduced use of restrictive practices are outlined. As much of this work has been conducted with other populations, such as people with mental health needs and the elderly, these findings will be translated into an intellectual disability context where necessary. In order to try and merge what might otherwise be seen as complementary, but potentially separate work streams, the possible role of PBS in helping deliver these necessary organisational conditions will then be explored. Finally, a suggested project template for reducing restrictive practices in an organisation will be described. The overall aim is to help services who wish to reduce their use of restrictive procedures to do so in practice.

Though the use of physical intervention and, more specifically restraint, has probably received the greatest attention to date, it is of course only one form of restrictive practice. Therefore, this publication will also make reference to the use of seclusion and as required medication. For clarity, the following definitions of each of these restrictive management strategies are provided at the outset:

Physical restraint:

Physical restraint has been defined as:

'... any method of responding to challenging behaviour which involves some degree of direct physical force to limit or restrict movement of mobility.' (Harris et al, 2000)

Restraint can either be:

- personal (ie, applied by one or more persons restricting the movement of another)

- mechanical (ie, achieved by the use of some sort of device or apparatus, such as splints or harnesses)

- environmental (ie, achieved by certain restrictions in the environment, such as locked doors)

Seclusion:

The Code of Practice for the Mental Health Act (2008) in England defines seclusion as:

'... the supervised containment of a person[1] in a room, which may be locked. Its sole aim is to contain severely disturbed behaviour which is likely to cause harm to others.' (Department of Health, 2008)

Rapid tranquillisation/as required medication:

Rapid tranquillisation is defined as 'the use of medication to calm/lightly sedate the service user and reduce the risk to self and/or others'. Its aim is:

[1] The Mental Health Act Code of Practice uses the term 'patient'

'... to achieve an optimal reduction in agitation and aggression, thereby allowing a thorough psychiatric evaluation to take place, whilst allowing comprehension and response to spoken messages throughout.' (NICE, 2005)

Pro re nata or PRN (as needed or as required) medication is often used in a similar way to rapid tranquillisation with people who have intellectual disabilities and challenging behaviour

In terms of general terminology, 'intellectual disability' has been preferred to 'learning disability' throughout.

2. The use and impact of restrictive practices on people who have intellectual disabilities

How often are restrictive management strategies employed with people who have intellectual disabilities?

Though the literature in this area is fairly sparse, it provides a consistent perspective about the use of restrictive practices in UK services for people with intellectual disabilities:

- Lowe et al (2005), in an administrative population study carried out in South Wales, found that restraint was used with between 39–45 per cent of children and 17–36 per cent of adults depending on the severity of their presenting challenging behaviour. Seclusion was used with around a quarter of children, and at slightly lower rates with adults. In contrast, the use of medication to sedate behaviour was reported in 42 per cent of extremely challenging adults and only 6 per cent in the equivalent child group.

- Emerson (2002) reported the use of restraint for 28–67 per cent of children and 8–57 per cent of adults with intellectual disability and challenging behaviour based on the analysis of data from a series of epidemiological studies conducted in the North West of England. The equivalent figures for seclusion were 32–68 per cent and 15–39 per cent, and 1–6 per cent and 15–35 per cent for emergency sedation.

- In a study of congregate and non-congregate services for adults with challenging behaviour in England and Wales, Robertson et al (2005) looked at the use of restrictive practices for service users at two points in time. Averaged across these two data points, emergency sedation was used for 27 per cent users in non-congregate settings and 38 per cent in congregate settings. The equivalent figures for seclusion were 37 per cent and 46 per cent, restraint by one member of staff 17 per cent and 46 per cent, and restraint by two or more members of staff 21 per cent and 53 per cent.

- In a survey of NHS, local authority, third sector and private residential services for adults in South-East England, Deveau and McGill (2009) found that almost 50 per cent of respondents reported using some form of physical intervention and one third physical interventions that were more restrictive.

- Using data from the 2007 National Audit Survey of people living in over 500 NHS and independent sector facilities in England, Sturmey (2009) reported that 53 per cent used some form of restraint, 80 per cent used as required (PRN) medication, and just over 10 per cent seclusion. Physical restraint use was far more common than mechanical restraint use (45 per cent vs 6 per cent).

Both individually and collectively, these studies present a very concerning picture. Given that many services for people with intellectual disabilities often use informal interventions (ie, ones that have not been sanctioned by appropriate professionals or documented in formal care plans), it is however possible that these figures actually underestimate the use of restrictive interventions in practice. For example, in a Canadian study by Feldman et al, (2004), out of over 2,500 interventions reported, 27 per cent were concerned with restrictive practices; 63 per cent of the latter were informal, and 43 per cent of these were assessed as being dangerous. Similarly, the Mental Health Act Commission (MHAC) in the UK has drawn attention to the fact that the use of seclusion may be under-reported by virtue of it being euphemistically described in other ways (such as 'removal from the environment', 'de-escalation rooms', 'removal to a calming room', 'placed in a quiet room' and so on) (MHAC, 2006, p 310).

Some UK data are also available regarding the use of restrictive management strategies in family settings. For example, Adams and

Allen (2001) reported that parental physical intervention was the most common response to aggressive behaviour in 56 per cent of children referred to a specialist behavioural intervention team, while a national survey (Allen et al, 2006) found that 88 per cent of parents reported using physical intervention with their children at some point and that 21 per cent did so frequently. Personal restraint was most common in the latter study, but mechanical and environmental restraints were also reported. Only a quarter of parents had received training in reactive behaviour management, and many of the physical interventions used had therefore been improvised and were highly risky; these included, for example, using headlocks; prone restraint; and applying additional body weight to the child's back. Only 4 per cent reported using environmental restrictions that could be viewed as equivalent to seclusion; these strategies included shutting the child in a bedroom, locking doors, putting the child in a cupboard and using a stable door for containment. Qualitative research by Elford et al (2010) also identified the use of physical restraint, mechanical restraint, seclusion and as required medication in family settings.

What factors predict the use of restrictive practices?

What do we know about who is most likely to experience restrictive practices? Again, there is a limited literature that has attempted to explore this question. Reporting on a series of studies, Emerson (2002) found that personal risk factors associated with increased use of restrictive practices included: increased severity of intellectual impairment/adaptive behaviour; having communicative difficulties; age (younger age in adults with restraint, older age in children with seclusion); being male; coming from a minority ethnic background; and having diagnoses of autism or mental health problems. Environmental risk factors included: attending a special school; living in residential care; not attending a day service; living in a residence with less normal architectural features; and higher staffing levels and service user numbers.

11

Robertson et al (2005) found that restraint use was strongly correlated with whether or not staff had been trained in physical intervention in the previous three years. They also reported that medication use was associated with increased service user mobility and a body mass index indicative of obesity. McGill et al (2009) found that individuals who experienced restraint, seclusion or emergency medication were more likely to be male, young, not subject to legal detention, and to be described as having autistic spectrum disorder.

Allen et al, (2009) reported that restraint use was predicted by the presence of destructive behaviour, having behavioural plans in place for specific forms of challenging behaviour, detention under mental health legislation and lower levels of adaptive behaviour. The use of seclusion was linked with having more severe challenging behaviour, the presence of destructive behaviour and being placed in a service away from the person's area of origin. Finally, sedation was associated with detention under mental health legislation and having behavioural plans in place for specific forms of challenging behaviour. In addition, younger participants were more likely to be restrained and older participants to receive emergency medication. People who were restrained were also likely to experience both seclusion and sedation.

In family settings, Allen et al (2006) found that the frequency of physical intervention use was positively correlated with likelihood of child injury and severity of challenging behaviour and negatively correlated with parental age.

A few studies have restricted themselves to institutional populations. In contrast to the studies described above, Sturmey (1999) found only limited evidence that between-participant differences in challenging behaviour were predictive of restraint use. In a replication of the 1999 study however, Sturmey et al (2005) found that higher scores on the Impulse and Elimination Disorder sub-scales of the Diagnostic Assessment for the Severely Handicapped-II (Matson, 1995) and on the Irritability sub-scale of the Aberrant Behaviour Checklist (Aman et al, 1985) predicted which people were restrained.

Mason (1996) reported that, in a special hospital for individuals with very high-risk behaviours and forensic needs, people with intellectual disability tended to be secluded more frequently than individuals without. Interestingly, the behaviours leading to seclusion often did not appear sufficiently severe to warrant the application of this procedure and the people concerned often responded badly to its application. Rangecroft et al (1997) also found that many of those secluded in a hospital setting had severe intellectual disability.

Leggett and Sylvester (2003) found that women in a secure unit were more likely to be secluded and less likely to receive medication. They also discovered that the use of seclusion was associated with causal explanations that carers attributed for challenging behaviour, it being more likely when carers believed that the service user could have done something to avoid the incident if they wished, and also when they felt that it was unlikely that the staff member could have done anything to do so. The use of emergency medication was associated with a belief that the service user could not have done anything to avoid the incident, but only with male service users. Staff were less likely to be able to give explanations for the use of seclusion with women. Dagnan and Weston (2006) found that there was no association between attributional measures and reactive management options chosen, but that physical intervention was much more likely to be used in response to physical rather than verbal aggression.

In general, though the above literature makes some reference to carer and organisational variables, in the main it has tried to explain what makes the use of restrictive practices more likely simply by exploring characteristics of service users. For this reason, the predictive power of the variables identified in most studies has, perhaps not surprisingly, not been particularly strong.

13

In contrast, studies on violence in the work place have suggested that such behaviour is best understood via a systemic model that includes user, carer, organisational and external influences (Bowie, 1996; Paterson et al, 2008). Whether or not restrictive practices are used is likely to be similarly determined by a complex equation that includes organisational policy and culture, staff training, resources, individual staff competencies and staff attitudes, in addition to characteristics of the people being served. As will be described later, efforts to reduce the use of such practices are congruent with this perspective in that they have tended to focus more on changing organisational rather than personal characteristics.

What impacts do restrictive practices have?

Despite the huge emphasis that training in physical intervention is given in the UK, data on its effectiveness is conspicuously absent. Allen (2001) surveyed the available literature and examined a range of outcomes that included participant knowledge; participant confidence; competence in performing physical interventions; impact on rates of challenging behaviour; rates of use of reactive procedures; and injury rates to users and staff. The research outcomes were at best equivocal and very few studies of any methodological quality were identified. A further review by McDonnell in 2009 suggested that little had altered in the period between these two publications.

We therefore lack evidence to suggest that such training is effective in managing risk behaviours, or that it improves safety for service users or safety for carers. We similarly lack any substantial robust data on the effectiveness of seclusion or as required medication (Baker et al, 2007; Hilton and Whiteford, 2008; Muralidharan and Fenton, 2006; Nelstrop et al, 2006; Paton et al, 2008; Sailas and Fenton, 2000; Whicher et al, 2002); this is true both in general and in particular with people who have intellectual disabilities. There is also significant concern about the use of regularly prescribed psychotropic medication to manage challenging behaviour in people with intellectual disability given a similar lack of evidence for its efficacy (Kennedy and Meyer, 1998; Tyrer et al, 2008; Deb et al, 2009; Matson and Neal, 2009; Unwin and Deb, 2010) and concerns that it may be administered in the absence of clear outcome objectives or monitoring of side effects (Marshall, 2004).

Concern about the lack of evidence for the primary intended effects of restrictive practices is further heightened by the risk of potential side effects. With restraint, these include physical harm ranging from minor injury to death. With sedation, they may involve confusion, extra-pyramidal side effects, weight gain, postural hypotension, metabolic abnormalities and stroke. Physical abuse, verbal abuse and emotional harm (recurring trauma, nightmares, etc.) have all been reported in relation to restraint and seclusion. Though the relevant literature is essentially descriptive in nature, such effects are well documented and appear to generalise across different user populations and settings (Allen, 2008).

Summary

Adding the above studies together, the summary position in UK services for people with intellectual disability would appear to be that we are using procedures that have a very questionable evidence base for their effectiveness (in terms of making people safe and managing difficult behaviour), but which raise significant questions about side effects (in terms of causing potential physical and emotional distress), at very high rates.

A logical conclusion regarding any intervention that had these characteristics would be that urgent work should be undertaken to limit and, where possible, eradicate its use. The next section goes on to consider what is known about how to achieve such outcomes with regard to the use of restrictive practices.

3. Initiatives to reduce restrictive practice

Two broad forms of intervention to achieve reductions in the use of restrictive practice have been described in the literature. The first covers reduction of restrictive practice in individual or small groups of service users; this work is located essentially within the behavioural literature and typically follows an experimental format. The second covers more widespread, whole organisation attempts at reduction and these generally follow a more descriptive, quasi-experimental approach. Summary interventions and outcomes from both approaches will be briefly presented below.

Individual user level

Two recent reviews (Luiselli, 2009; Williams, 2010) have looked at some of the critical findings regarding the use of behavioural interventions to reduce the use of restraint with people who have intellectual disability. These have concluded that:

- procedures to reduce restraint use need to be implemented strategically and at an early stage in interventions for people who challenge so as to reduce carer reliance upon them

- changing antecedent triggers for behaviour and interrupting early stages of behavioural escalation can effectively reduce the reactive use of restraint

- changing the criteria for releasing individuals from restraint can also reduce its use. Specifically, this involves releasing people from restraint after a set time period (for example, one minute) as opposed to applying restraint until the person calms (which would be normal practice in most services)

- successful procedures for the fading of mechanical restraint for self-injury have been repeatedly demonstrated

- long-term follow-up is required to assess the results of reduction efforts

- individual or small group efforts to reduce restraint use will be more effective if they are embedded within broader organisational initiatives of the type described in the section that follows

Encouraging though the results of these reviews are, with the exception of studies on fading mechanical restraint, they are based on a very small number of case studies; in general, they have also involved younger individuals as participants (who may accordingly be smaller and less physically challenging). They nevertheless offer promise in terms of being able to reduce restraint use and the initial findings about using time-based criteria for restraint release could be very significant in reducing risk from prolonged restraint application. However, further work is required in all these areas.

On a slightly different theme, Singh et al (2009) have demonstrated that staff-based interventions can also significantly impact on rates of restraint and as required medication use. In this study, 23 staff working in four group homes took part in a 12-session mindfulness training course that included instruction in non-judgemental acceptance of service users and meditation. Staff and user injuries, as well as restraint and medication use, all reduced to near zero levels by the end of study period. Using a similar methodology, Singh at al (2006) also reported major reductions in restraint use following mindfulness training for 15 staff working in three group homes. Noone and Hastings (2009) described how a similar mindfulness intervention (Acceptance and Commitment Therapy) could bring about reductions in staff stress, but did not measure whether this resulted in beneficial consequential impacts for service users. Again, while this work is highly promising, it is limited to a very small number of studies at the present time.

Organisational level

Organisational initiatives to reduce restrictive practices have a very long history. In the 18th and 19th centuries, pioneers such as Jean-Baptist Pussin and Philippe Pinel in France, John Conolly in England and Dorothea Dix in the United States all promoted reductions in the use of, and alternatives to, mechanical restraint as part of wider reforms of institutional care of people with mental ill health.

In each case, systems-wide organisational change was a key aspect of the change strategies employed. For example, Pussin and Pinel's interventions at the Bicêtre in Paris involved the introduction of a new therapeutic approach involving close contact with, and observation of, patients and the cessation of bleeding, purging and blistering, as well as the abolition of iron shackles and straightjackets. Much of Dix's work involved gathering data on the care of people with mental health problems and then using these to argue for legislative changes, but she was also involved in the provision of heating and clothing to inmates at various institutions as well as calling for reductions in restraint use.

The fact that the concerns first raised several centuries ago have not been adequately addressed is illustrated by what Masters (2008) calls the *Pinel Test*: He describes this as follows:

'… if we could bring Dr Pinel to America and show him modern inventions, like the automobile, the airplane, the television, the computer, or even the electric light, he would likely be amazed. However, show him a current piece of mechanical restraint equipment or someone doing a physical hold, or even a seclusion room, he would be able to observe, "Oh, yes we used those, or we had that."'
(Masters, 2008, p 45)

The fact that current approaches to the use of restrictive practices do not pass the Pinel test is evidence of the failure to adopt systemic approaches to reducing the use of such strategies in human services.

However, there are a number of contemporary accounts of how such reductions could be achieved.

Huckshorn (2005) identifies six core strategies for restraint and seclusion reduction:

- Leadership
  The critical contribution of leadership to any organisational change strategy is self-evidential. In relation to the reduction of use of restrictive strategies, this leadership involves: having this reduction goal clearly enshrined in mission statements; producing a clear plan that targets this objective; having senior management sign this and each subsequent stage off as a core organisational activity; creating reduction champions at various levels of the organisation and having recognition events to acknowledge staff achievements; and clearly delegating reduction tasks and holding people as accountable for their actions via routine reports and reviews.

- Using data to inform practice
  Data-driven practice is also critical to reducing restrictive practices. This involves constructing a baseline of current use and then using these data to set goals for improved performance that are communicated widely to the staff team. The data should be used to promote healthy competition between different service units, but not punitively with those that may lag behind in results terms (eg, to inform disciplinary action). Data should allow for the identification of particular usage patterns (eg, by staff member, time of day, location) and the assessment of collateral impacts (eg, staff and service user injury, use of emergency medication), and be subject to frequent review by executive management.

- Workforce development
  Staff training is clearly a necessary but not sufficient intervention for organisational change. In this context, workforce development should include: clear orientation to the organisational objective; key

aspects of underpinning theories described above (and particularly service user experience of restrictive practices); core skills in building therapeutic relationships; non-confrontational boundary setting; instruction in safe, ethical restrictive practices; the importance of monitoring vital signs during their use; the empowerment of staff in being able to modify agreed rules in the face of dealing with real-life events; and the need to learn from and address any such recurring events in a multi-disciplinary forum.

- Use of specific reduction tools
  There are a number of tools or procedures that can support the reduction agenda. These include: the use of proven assessment tools to identify users who pose a higher risk of violence; individual assessments of the physical health status of users to identify those with pre-existing physical health or emotional health problems that may counter-indicate the use of specific restrictive procedures; proactive emergency management plans that anticipate commonly occurring scenarios at both service and individual levels; changes to the therapeutic environment (eg, the development of calming and sensory rooms); and the introduction of meaningful activities.

- Service user involvement
  The involvement of service users, their relatives and advocates is also seen as essential to the initiative and can be achieved via membership of key committees and working groups; conducting regular satisfaction surveys and acting on their results; and having service users fulfil specific roles within the organisation.

- Debriefing strategies
  There are two forms of debriefing that can contribute to reducing restrictive practices. Immediate post-incident debriefing by senior staff aims to ensure the safety of all those involved in a violent incident, that necessary documentation is completed and that a safe and calm environment is re-established. More formal debriefing will typically occur some days later utilising tools, such

as, root cause analysis (RCA) in order to gain a deeper understanding of the critical factors that lead to the incident; how similar incidents can be prevented in future; and to make sure that traumatic consequences are minimised for both service users and carers.

Bullard et al (2003), in a publication from the Child Welfare League of America, identified leadership, organisational culture (and notably, the development of a person-centred focus), agency policies, staff training, treatment environment and continuous quality improvement as critical to reducing restrictive practices. They also discuss the potential for the elimination of restrictive practices by mandatory policy changes, and indicate that a number of controversial procedures (notably basket-holds and floor restraint) have been prohibited in some states, often following fatalities involving service users. As the authors observe, it is critical when eliminating procedures by mandate to ensure that proscribing one procedure (eg, prone restraint) does not result in collateral increases in others (eg, seclusion or as required medication). This report also stresses the need to develop individualised behaviour support plans for any child with a recorded history of requiring physical intervention; as the primary focus of such plans is prevention of challenging behaviours, they are potentially a major tool in reduction strategies.

Colton (2004) has synthesised the major themes of all these documents and incorporated them into a single checklist for assessing organisational readiness for reducing restrictive practices. It covers nine themes of: leadership, orientation and training, staffing, environmental factors, programmatic structure, timely and responsive treatment planning, debriefing, communication and consumer involvement and systems evaluation and quality improvement. Used as a baseline measure, its primary function is to help identify the gaps between current and desired performance. It is not intended to be used for benchmarking, given that this may be a punitive process for low-performing organisations; instead, it is designed to be used as a tool on a repeated basis in order to capture change across organisations committed to reducing restrictive practices. As such, it aims to contribute to, as well as assess, cultural change.

Though the above work focuses primarily on restraint, many authors also report their application to reducing seclusion use, thus suggesting that organisation interventions of this type have a generalised impact (eg, Gaskin et al, 2007; Crosland et al, 2008; Delaney, 2006; Donat, 2002, 2005; Martin et al, 2008; Smith et al, 2005).

The literature on reducing as required medication is generally less extensive and limited for the most part to non-intellectually disabled populations, but it too allows for some general practice principles to be described (Baker et al, 2008; Bisconer et al, 1995; Dean et al, 2009; Crosland et al, 2008; Donat, 2002, 2005; Patrick et al, 2006; Rowland and Treece, 2000; Singh and Winter, 1984; Spirrison and Grosskopf, 1991; Thomas et al, 2006). Interventions to reduce as required medication use in service settings have therefore included:

- Introducing better data-based review procedures
- Involvement of very senior clinical and administrative staff in the monitoring and review process
- Establishment of specific task groups to monitor data
- The development of early identification and review procedures for high risk users
- The introduction of individualised behavioural support plans for affected users
- The introduction of good practice standards
- Staff training
- Provision of access to skilled experts
- Provision of activity programmes for users

Again, these interventions have significant overlap with those recommended for use in reducing the use of restraint and seclusion, further reinforcing the notion that it is possible to identify a suite of organisational initiatives that are likely to have a common impact across all three forms of restrictive practice.

Outcome data on whole-organisation approaches

The six core restraint and reduction strategies referred to above are reported to have been widely implemented in North America in services for both children and adults with mental health needs. Huckshorn (2004) refers to data from pilot testing in eight states that resulted in 63 per cent showing reduced restraint and 71 per cent reduced seclusion hours, with 88 per cent restraining and 86 per cent secluding fewer service users, 72 per cent having reduced restraint events and 100 per cent reduced seclusion events. Not all procedures were in use in all settings however, so the denominator was not common across these figures. Overall, restrictive practice hours were reduced by as much as 79 per cent, the percentage of people subject to such procedures by up to 62 per cent and the number of events resulting in their use by as much as 68 per cent. The current author has not been able to locate this original data however.

There are numerous descriptive accounts that appear essentially supportive of the importance of the organisational change strategies that contribute to reducing restrictive practice. Colton (2008), for example, conducted interviews with five separate inpatient/residential services for children and adolescents that had achieved successful reduction in an effort to identify critical independent variables involved. The importance of leadership, planned programme change and improving the treatment environment were highlighted in these services. Thompson et al (2008) reported on salient variables in the achievement of an 89 per cent reduction in restraint use in a 41-bed residential service for youths with mental health needs. Five hundred and sixty one individuals used the service over the study period. The primary intervention in this case was educational, with staff receiving training that stressed the importance of proactive approaches to difficult behaviour, non-violent de-escalation strategies and the development of self-control procedures. Carter et al (2008) described an intervention that included introducing data-driven practice, changing agency culture, providing additional training and modifying individual treatment plans in a Canadian service supporting children with mental health needs in residential, day treatment and off-site programmes. The intervention reportedly achieved a 50 per cent reduction in restraint use over a 12-month period. Ryan et al (2008) described the impact of a multi-faceted intervention strategy that included staff surveys, training in conflict de-escalation and physical intervention, and greater emphasis on data-driven practice on 42 individuals in a school for students with emotional and behaviour disorders. Restraint use decreased by 39.4 per cent, but time-out use increased by 10 per cent.

Recent years have also seen three major reviews of interventions to reduce restrictive practices with three service user groups that help shed light on what might be the key independent variables in this process. First, Evans, Wood and Lambert (2002) reviewed 16 studies on restraint reduction in acute and residential care; inclusion criteria were that the study population was an adult one, located in one of the two specified care settings, and reported outcomes that included restraint use, falls, injury or psychotropic medication use. Despite also having a randomised controlled trial as an inclusion criterion, only one such study was identified and therefore controlled trials, pre-post studies and case studies were all also included. Sixteen studies were discussed in the final review, the focus of which was essentially on the use of mechanical restraint with elderly and other in-patient groups in receipt of nursing care. Second, a descriptive review by Delaney (2006) looked at the evidence base for the reduction of both seclusion and restraint in child and adolescent psychiatric in-patient units; it also briefly considered the use of as required medication use. Inclusion criteria were that the study should be less than 10 years old, focused on children, data-based and written in English or having an English translation available. Third, Gaskin, Elsom and Happell (2007) conducted a more systematic review looking at initiatives to reduce seclusion in psychiatric facilities. This study identified 16 studies that met the inclusion criteria of being published within the last 20 years, being data-based, having pre-post data on seclusion rates and employing interventions that were not simply restricted to medication changes. Although six of the studies identified were conducted in child or adolescent psychiatric service settings, only two of these studies cited were also cited by Delany (2006). Ten of the studies reviewed also included data on restraint as well as seclusion reduction.

Together, these reviews report 36 data-based outcomes of seclusion and/or restraint based outcomes. Evans et al (2002) report average reductions of 57 per cent (range 0–91 per cent) and Gaskin et al (2007) 62 per cent (range 26–100 per cent); the Delany (2006) review fails to present data in a form that can be adequately summarised but, for those papers where the data are cited, reductions of between 22 per cent to 'near zero' are reported. Although there are a small number of reported negative findings, the overall conclusions from these reviews are that substantial reductions in the use of restrictive practices can be achieved that are generalisable across different user populations, for both seclusion and restraint, and with different forms of the latter (ie personal and mechanical).

It is possible to identify some common characteristics of apparently successful reduction initiatives as described across these three reviews. Staff training, changes in policy and philosophy, the development of individualised assessments and interventions, and user participation are common to all. The need for committed leadership, the involvement of multi-disciplinary teams, the development of groups of staff with enhanced expertise in managing risk behaviours, the introduction of systematic data reviews and improving the service environment were mentioned by at least two. The formation of a specific restraint reduction task force and using additional pharmacological interventions were each mentioned only once.

Despite the fact that these reviews cover different populations and different forms of restrictive practice, substantial agreement is evident between them as to what constitutes the core ingredients of successful reduction strategies. Furthermore, there is significant correspondence between the critical ingredients suggested here and those identified by Huckshorn (2004) and Colton (2004). To some extent, this may be a tautological finding however as Huckshorn reports that the six core strategies programme was based on 'a thorough and ongoing review of available research and relevant literature' (p 27). Colton similarly states that his checklist is based on 'a review of more than 80 publications and Internet resources' (p 4). While the conclusion that further reviews support these principles should not be surprising, they provide a useful corroboration of the above analyses.

Although the results from these reviews are encouraging, the limitations of the studies concerned are significant. With one exception, they are at best quasi-experimental and the impacts of independent variables on dependent variables can therefore only be implied. A further complication is that most studies feature complex, multi-faceted organisational interventions, thus making it difficult to identify critical dependent variables. It is the contention of Gaskill et al (2007) that none of these individual components would be sufficiently powerful in isolation to achieve the kind of outcomes described above, but that, despite the weaknesses in experimental design, the cumulative weight of the studies in this area provide strong evidence that the use of restrictive practices in service settings can be substantially reduced. This seems a sensible conclusion at the present time.

Though organisational initiatives to reduce restrictive practice in the field of intellectual disabilities have been reported on a smaller scale to date (eg, Allen et al, 1997), some larger-scale projects are also now in evidence. Sturmey and McGlynn (2003) report on two examples. In the first, targeted multi-disciplinary team work, generalised staff instruction (involving empathy building, alternatives to restraint, etc.), individualised training and the introduction of specific restraint reduction targets achieved significant reductions in mechanical restraint (though not in physical restraint), and maintenance or as required medication in a large institutional facility. In the second, an organisational behaviour management initiative (involving enhanced data collection, enhanced supervision and monitoring, verbal and graphical feedback), demonstrated significant reductions for 20 out of 22 users who were resident in another institutional facility. Sanders (2009) similarly reported on how a 99.4 per cent reduction in restraint use and reduction in staff injuries in a residential facility serving 75 children and 45 adults with autism and/or intellectual disability was achieved through an intervention that involved seeking staff input as active participants, training, increased management support and increased monitoring.

Perhaps one of the largest scale attempts to change restrictive practices to date is that underway in Victoria, Australia. Backed by the legislation of the Disability Act (2006), which requires that the use of any restraint or seclusion must be included in a behaviour support plan, the Office of the Senior Practitioner has developed a sophisticated database for monitoring restrictive practice and behaviour plan use and quality that is employed on a state-wide basis (Department of Human Services, 2010). The Office also develops guidelines and standards, provides education, gives support to agencies in developing behavioural support plans and undertakes research. As this is a fairly recent initiative, outcome data are not yet available on the efficacy of this programme.

Summary

Though there is a lack of robust experimental evidence, there is significant practice-based evidence to suggest that restrictive practices can be reduced across a variety of user groups and settings. Analysis of the key ingredients of successful reduction programmes suggests that it is possible to identify critical strategies that appear to be common to efforts to reduce the use of restraint, seclusion and as required medications. In summary, these are as follows:

- Leadership

- Consumer involvement

- Development of acceptable environments

- Development of good programmatic structure

- Individualised, proactive intervention planning

- Clear crisis management strategies

- Staffing

- Workforce development and training

- Processing after the event

- Data-driven practice and quality assurance

At present, it is not possible to determine which of these strategies are critical to such efforts. It is therefore best to assume that all are necessary, and none sufficient, components for change. In the next section, the goodness of fit between these strategies and PBS as a service model will be considered.

4. The potential role of positive behavioural support in reducing restrictive practices

As mentioned in the introduction, BILD recently changed its agenda from focussing on physical interventions to positive behavioural support (PBS). Further to its 2009 conference, it issued the mission statement shown in Table 1 in order to reflect that change:

Table 1: BILD's PBS mission

1. Make sure that all people with learning disabilities can exercise their human rights and be valued members of their local communities.
2. Focus on vulnerable and disadvantaged groups including:
   - People with complex needs
   - People from black and minority ethnic communities
   - People with autism
   - Offenders and those in the judicial system.
3. Work in partnership with families, carers, friends and the key individuals in people's lives.
4. Ensure that people's individual communication needs are positively addressed.
5. Develop and promote an evidence base for practice.
6. Develop a framework of good practice guidance that focuses on positive behaviour support and person-centred planning.
7. Identify, disseminate and promote good practice in reducing the use of restrictive practices and the implementation of positive behaviour support.
8. Educate all stakeholders that the use of restrictive practices is potentially dangerous.
9. Eliminate the use of unnecessary restrictive and aversive practice.
10. Ensure that appropriate training and learning opportunities are available for all staff and supporters.

Though it constitutes a powerful statement of intent, the mission statement does not say a great deal about PBS per se and so it is worth doing so for readers who may be unfamiliar with this approach.

The therapeutic model that is now known as PBS emerged from the often vitriolic debate on the use of aversive behavioural procedures that took place in the late 1980s to early 1990s (eg, Axelrod, 1990; Donellan and LaVigna, 1990; Linscheid and Landau, 1993; Meyer and Berkman, 1993) and which, in some quarters, is still continuing (Foxx, 2005; Mulick and Butter, 2005). Central to this debate was the high frequency of use of punitive behavioural interventions and the nature of the stimuli used in such interventions (Guess et al, 1987). One suggested contributing factor to this situation was the lack of an overall values base to guide the application of technologies derived from the field of applied behaviour analysis (Emerson and McGill, 1989). Positive behaviour support addresses this deficit by combining the tools of behavioural intervention with the values base of social role valorisation (and its emphasis on achieving community presence, participation, increased respect, improving relationships and developing personal competencies) and the individual focus of person-centred planning. As such, it fits well with the aspirations of all national policy statements for people with learning disabilities within the UK.

Although its central theoretical model is clearly behavioural, PBS is also an inclusive approach that blends best practice from several theoretical perspectives into a coherent intervention model. This is captured in the following definition which states that PBS is:

'... characterised by educational, proactive and respectful interventions that involve teaching alternative skills to problem behaviours and changing problematic environments. It blends best practices in behavioural technology, educational methods and ecological systems change with person-centred values in order to achieve outcomes that are meaningful to the individual and to his or her family.' (Bambara et al, 2004)

Positive behaviour support is predicated on an understanding of why, when and how challenging behaviour happens, and what purpose it serves for the person. This is achieved via the process of functional assessment. Evidence shows that conducting such pre-intervention assessment significantly improves intervention outcomes (Campbell, 2003; Carr et al, 1999; Didden et al, 1997, 2006; Scotti et al, 1991; Harvey et al, 2009). A data-driven approach is therefore implicit in PBS. As well as being crucial to understanding behaviour, data collection is central to assessing the impact of PBS interventions.

Positive behaviour support rejects the use of aversive behavioural approaches and focuses instead on altering triggers for behaviour (in order to reduce the likelihood of the behaviour occurring) and skill teaching (as a lack of critical skills in key areas such as communication is often a significant contributory factor to the development of behavioural challenges). The former strategies might include altering known conditions that increase the probability of challenging behaviour occurring (eg, environmental factors such as space and light; social factors such as the number of people in a setting; programmatic factors such as activity levels; and intra-personal factors such as mental health needs and drug regimes etc.) or changing specific triggers for behaviour (eg, modifying instructional methods, interpersonal style, reducing demands, increasing choice). Bearing these possibilities in mind, Active Support (Jones et al, 1999) is potentially an important component within a PBS framework and there is some emerging evidence that the introduction of this form of programmatic intervention (Bradshaw et al, 2004; Beadle-Brown et al, 2008; Toogood et al, 2009) and that programmatic changes in general (Carr et al, 1999) can reduce challenging behaviour and enhance the impact of PBS interventions. Skill-based interventions could involve teaching general skills (as the more skilled someone is, the less likely it is that they will have to resort to using challenging behaviour in order to get their needs met), teaching functionally equivalent skills (skills that serve exactly the same purpose as the challenging behaviour; for example, using a communication board to signal to carers when you want a drink rather than throwing objects to do so), functional similar skills (ones that achieve the same outcome, but via different means; for example, learning to make a drink independently) or coping skills (such as controlled breathing and relaxation) to help people cope better with common stressors in their lives. Achieving changes in quality of life is therefore both an intervention and outcome measure and behaviour change is achieved as a side-effect of the use of these constructive, developmental strategies.

Reflecting the multiple influences on behaviour and the multiple actions that may be needed to address the causal factors concerned, PBS interventions typically have several strands. Importantly, while PBS majors on preventative strategies for changing behaviour, it also incorporates reactive strategies for managing such behaviours when they occur.

Using the model of primary prevention (changing aspects of a person's living and working environment to reduce the likelihood that challenging behaviour will occur), secondary prevention (spotting signs of behavioural agitation early and intervening early so as to prevent further escalation) and reactive strategies (pre-planned safe, ethical and effective responses to challenging behaviours that cannot be prevented) (Allen et al, 1997), the summary tools of PBS are shown in Table 2.

Table 2: Some core PBS strategies

Primary prevention	Changing features of person's physical environment Altering programmatic environment Introducing total communication Addressing internal setting events (mental and physical health)

	Improving carer confidence and competence Eliminating or modifying specific triggers for behaviour Increasing rates of access to preferred reinforcers Increasing the density of social contact Increasing rates of engagement Modifying demands Providing additional help Embedding Building behavioural momentum Teaching general skills Teaching functionally equivalent skills Teaching coping skills
Secondary prevention	Stimulus change Stimulus removal Prompting to coping skills Not ignoring Strategic capitulation Diversion to reinforcing activities Diversion to compelling activities
Reactive strategies	Proxemics Self-protective Minimal restraint

It is beyond the scope of the current publication to discuss these in more detail, but interested readers are referred to Donnellan et al (1988); Meyer and Evans (1989); Durand (1990); McBrien and Felce (1992); Carr et al (1994); Zarkowska and Clements (1996); O'Neil et al (1997); and LaVigna and Willis (2003) for further information. Accredited, vocationally based e-learning training that expands on all these concepts is also available (further details of which can be obtained from joanne.wheeler@wales.nhs.uk).

In contrast to the position with restrictive practices, there is a solid data base that shows that behavioural interventions which do not use aversive approaches are for the most part as effective as those that do (Carr et al, 1999; Campbell, 2003; Didden et al, 1997, 2006; Harvey et al, 2009; Hsen-Hsing Ma, 2009; Scotti et al, 1991; Marquis et al, 2000; Scotti et al, 1996; Whitaker, 1993). Regarding PBS interventions specifically, Carr et al's (1999) meta-analysis of existing research to that point in time concluded that these alone produced 90 per cent or more reductions in challenging behaviours from baseline levels in 52 per cent of interventions and 80 per cent or more in 68 per cent of interventions.

Positive behaviour support also attends to the needs of those typically charged with implementing such strategies and the organisational supports required to deliver and maintain it over time. This is reflected in concepts such as:

- mediator analysis, whereby the strengths and needs of those charged with implementing PBS interventions are taken into account as a component of intervention design (Allen, 1999).

- competency based training programmes, such as the three-stage model of training described by LaVigna et al (1994) which involves establishing verbal competence (being able to describe what needs to be done), role play competence (demonstrating the ability to perform what needs to be done in role play) and in vivo competence (demonstrating the ability to perform what needs to be done whist working with the person displaying behavioural challenges).

- assessment of the goodness of fit between what intervention agents are being asked to do and their capacity and competence to do so (Albin et al, 1996).

- quality assurance systems such as the Periodic Service Review (LaVigna et al, 1994) that help ensure that PBS plans are implemented in practice and reliably achieve their intended outcomes.

Each of these organisational supports can be as crucial to the success of PBS interventions as the development of effective functional assessment and comprehensive individual plans. This is particularly so given that interventions are generally more successful if implemented by a person's normal carers rather than by external specialists (Carr et al, 1999) and successful interventions typically need to be maintained in the long-term if recovery of behaviour to baseline levels is to be avoided.

Positive behavioural support as a restraint reduction tool?

In the previous section, the characteristics of successful restrictive practice reduction strategies were reviewed. In this section, the characteristics of PBS have been outlined. It should already be apparent that there is a significant overlap between the two, and this is explored more formally in Table 3.

Table 3: Restrictive practice reduction strategies compared to PBS as a service system

Variable	Descriptor	PBS
Leadership	Identifying reduction of restrictive practice as an organisational priority that requires commitment at all levels.	Should be a given in any organisation seeking to adopt the systemic application of PBS as a clinical model. Implicit assumption in model.
Consumer involvement	Involvement of consumers and families in assessment and intervention process.	Core feature √
Person-centred organisational culture	Putting the needs of the consumer at the forefront. Embracing supportive language; flexible individual support and having collaboration rather than compliance and control as an objective.	Core feature √

Variable	Descriptor	PBS
Development of acceptable environments	Increasing the quality of and reducing pollutants in living environments.	Core feature √
Programmatic structure	Maximising meaningful routines and activities, empowering decision making.	Core feature √
Individualised proactive intervention planning	Individualised behaviour change plans for each individual subject in receipt or at risk of restrictive practices.	Core feature √
Clear crisis management strategies	Clear, safe, pragmatic plans for responding to known risk behaviours.	Core feature √
Staffing	Appropriate levels of staff resource, deployed in the most effective ways to meet user need.	Does not deal with resourcing per se, but the optimum allocation of resources to support the implementation of PBS plans is often a core consideration. Goodness of fit surveys/mediator analysis are central to this.
Workforce training and development	Competency-based training in critical user-related skills.	Core feature √

Variable	Descriptor	PBS
Processing after the event	Learning from incidents at a variety of levels (eg, immediate debriefing, RCA etc); ensuring that the emotional aftermath of difficult incidents is effectively managed and supported.	Specific debriefing around incidents should be a feature of reactive component. Consideration should also be given to the delivery of mindfulness or other training that proactively enables carers to deal with predictable stressors.
Data-driven practice and quality assurance	The routine and system-wide use of data to inform practice, set intervention and improvement goals, review outcome effectiveness.	Ongoing data analysis is a core feature.

From this comparison, with one or two exceptions, the core features of PBS appear to map well onto those associated with effective interventions to reduce restrictive practice. In particular, the development of a person-centred approach, helpful environments, clear programmatic structures, individualised proactive and reactive plans, and data-driven practice are all staple ingredients of the PBS model. Likewise, as illustrated earlier, PBS places considerable emphasis on those charged with implementing interventions (via mediator analysis, training, goodness of fit, etc.) and this will inevitably involve consideration of the most effective deployment of resources to meet need. In service planning terms, this may manifest itself, for example, in terms of rostering staff to work at times when user need for support is greatest, rather than through inflexible shift patterns.

Less obvious perhaps are the points about leadership, consumer involvement and processing after the event. As the table suggests, senior leadership commitment will however be an essential prerequisite in any organisation seeking to introduce PBS as a whole-system approach; either implicitly or explicitly, this will involve management making a commitment to reducing the use of restrictive practices. The evidence suggests that an explicit commitment is however likely to be more powerful. Involving consumers as participants in PBS interventions is perhaps generally less well developed, though there are published examples of involving family members as full partners in constructing and implementing interventions (Koegel et al, 1996; Lucyshen et al, 2002) and one functional assessment tool (O'Neill et al, 1997) that is designed to be completed directly with service users. There have also been user friendly materials developed to help users understand reactive strategies (BILD, 2008) and psychotropic medication (Unwin and Deb, 2010) and these could be a valuable tool in involving service users with intellectual disabilities formally in programmes to reduce the use of restrictive practices. Including advocacy organisations in PBS initiatives would also be a very positive way forward.

The rationale for pointing out the congruity between using PBS as a whole-system model and effective strategies to reduce restrictive practices is not academic. Services for people with intellectual disability often struggle to integrate different theoretical intervention models into a single approach. It is potentially helpful to note therefore that implementing PBS robustly has a high probability of being able to impact on the use of restraint, seclusion and as required medication, as well as producing the quality of life and behavioural gains referred to earlier. In a time of financial austerity, it may also be helpful to think that positive results can be obtained by pursuing a single over-arching model rather than multiple models which may require multiple training investments.

Also, at an individual level, implementing PBS supports should result in reduced use of restrictive options. Though this has not been substantially measured in the PBS literature to date, it is an important dependent measure in a three-centre study currently being conducted by services in Wales, Sussex and Ireland.

Summary

In this section, the characteristics of PBS have been outlined and compared to those of effective programmes for reducing restrictive practices. The overlap between the two is clearly substantial and, in theory, implementing PBS as an intervention model should impact positively on the use of restrictive practices at both an individual and organisational level. In the next section, these various ideas will be brought together into a single project plan.

5. A project plan for reducing restrictive practices

It should be clear from what has been written so far that achieving any significant reductions in the use of restrictive practices for people with intellectual disabilities will not occur by chance. Instead, achieving such reductions will require a considerable organisational commitment and investment in project planning.

In traditional terms, projects are usually seen as temporary organisational structures that are created for the purpose of delivering one or more objectives. In this case, the objective is to obtain a reduction in the use of restrictive strategies. While such an initiative will certainly require substantial attention in the short-term, it is also likely to require ongoing attention and maintenance if returns to baseline levels of use are to be avoided. In other words, any restrictive practice reduction strategy needs to be planned with a view to it needing to stay in place in the long-term. This is to be expected, as what is being sought is, in effect, cultural change that may take several years to achieve its full effect (Colton, 2008).

How to decide if you need this approach?

There is clearly no point in taking a massive organisational hammer to crack what might be a small organisational nut. If an organisation only supports a small number of service users who challenge and who are sometimes exposed to restrictive practices, the way forward probably lies solely in developing individualised PBS plans for those concerned. The objective of reducing the use of restraint, seclusion or as required medication remains the same, but the scale is insufficient to merit a broader, organisational change type project as is outlined below.

However, if an organisation specialises in supporting people who challenge, that display the kind of individual risk factors described in Section 2 of this publication and is using restrictive practices at the kinds of rates described in the same section (say for over 25 per cent of those supported), then it is at high risk and probable that it is going to need to develop a formal project to affect changes on a significant scale.

Successful projects tend to have a number of characteristics. These include:

- Clear objectives and products

- Clear plans for achieving these objectives

- A clear allocation of resources necessary to achieve the same

- A process for quality control

- A specified start date

- Clearly specified stages with individual start and finish dates

- A specified finish

Conversely, unsuccessful projects tend to:

- Have an unclear rationale

- Lack ownership amongst key stakeholders (for example, senior managers or front line staff)

- Have end objectives or products that are not defined in sufficient detail

- Fail to identify, monitor and control project activities

- Incorrectly estimate the effort required to achieve the project's objectives

- Have too many objectives and too few resources

- Have no contingencies for work being interrupted or unpredictable events

- Be adversely affected by excessive bureaucratic requirements

In short, the old adage of failing to plan is planning to fail is undoubtedly true. As the literature described in this publication shows, it is possible to think about how PBS can be used as a central strategy in a project to reduce restrictive practices. While there may be a number of different ways to do this in practice, the following project template may prove useful as a starting point for organisations that fall into the high-risk category described above. Although the plan is laid out in stages, some of these stages will be sequential (for example, collecting baseline data should always precede stages 3–9), but others will be overlapping (for example, the stages referring to whole organisation training in PBS, developing bespoke interventions, and delivering appropriate reactive training will almost certainly do so). The exact relationship between each one will however vary from one organisational context to another, and so the template can be as flexible as required. What is critical is that each of the stages is properly captured and resourced within a project plan because, as discussed previously, our present knowledge suggests that all the stages are necessary, and none sufficient, to achieve change. The template attempts to combine good project management principles with the key ingredients of PBS and effective restraint reduction programmes. Reflecting basic goal planning principles, space is provided to enable a record to be made of what needs to be done (How we plan to do this?) together with identifying who will be responsible for completing necessary actions, by when and whether this objective is achieved as planned.

The template can be downloaded as a Word document from the BILD website at: www.bild.org.uk/behavioursupport/rrp

Stage 1. Committing the organisation

Key things to think about:	How we plan to do this?	By whom?	By when?	Date achieved
• Having a clear goal to reduce restrictive practices in the organisation's mission statement.				
• Designating someone as having primary responsibility for this initiative.				
• Establishing a long-term project group to oversee the implementation of the project that includes senior professional and administrative staff together with representatives of staff at all levels of the organisation who will act as programme champions.				
• Providing this team with sufficient resources to achieve the project goal.				
• Ensuring that this project team reports to the organisation's most senior management team at each stage of the project and that the programme is a standing item on their agenda.				
• Charging the group with completing the project plan and identifying a specific start date for the project overall and its separate stages.				
• Working with service users and advocacy organisations to achieve meaningful user participation in the project team.				

Stage 2. Collecting baseline and ongoing data

Key things to think about:	How we plan to do this?	By whom?	By when?	Date achieved

Before introducing other changes, collect robust data on:
  • frequency of use of restraint, seclusion and as required medication
  • duration of restraint and seclusion
  • total number of service users experiencing each form of restrictive practice
  • rates and severity of injury to service users and staff
  • names of staff members involved.
• Building in a system for checking on the reliability of such data.
• Establishing a mechanism for collating this data on a monthly basis and submitting to the project team.
• Using the data to set reduction goals.				

Stage 3. Conduct an environmental audit				
Key things to think about:	How we plan to do this?	By whom?	By when?	Date achieved
• Ensuring that known environmental triggers for aggressive service user behaviour (such as excessive heat, noise, over-crowding) are identified within the service and corrective steps taken to address them. • Ensuring that the basic fabric within the service (decoration, furniture) are as pleasant as possible and maintained on a regular basis. • Ensuring that any environmental adaptations required to help manage challenging behaviour (eg, having toughened materials) are in place.				

Stage 4. Ensure that the whole organisation is trained in the principles of PBS

Key things to think about:	How we plan to do this?	By whom?	By when?	Date achieved
• Making sure that all staff in the organisation have a core understanding of the principles and practices of PBS. *NB* If the training does not include active support, plan separately for this training to be delivered across the service. • That managers and leaders have a more in-depth understanding that incorporates organisational tools (such as the Periodic Service Review and goodness of fit) that are needed to support PBS in practice. • That staff charged with responsibility for conducting individualised assessment and intervention plans receive much more in-depth theoretical and practical training. • That refresher training and training for new recruits is built into the organisation's training plan. • That the training received and workplace practices and tools (eg, format for individual plans) are entirely congruent and reinforcing of one another.				

Stage 5. Ensure that all those in need of bespoke PBS assessment and intervention receive it				
Key things to think about:	How we plan to do this?	By whom?	By when?	Date achieved
Ensuring that for all service users in receipt of or at risk of receiving restrictive interventions: • There is an up-to-date functional assessment of their behaviour. • An individualised PBS plan that identifies environmental and individual triggers for challenging behaviour and clear steps to prevent or reduce the impacts of such triggers. • That the plan also specifies any skill teaching that needs to be put in place. • That the plan also specifies any necessary reactive strategies that may be required to manage common challenges that the user displays and which may not always be preventable. • That any risk assessments that these strategies are based on are accurate, reflect both current and historical patterns of behaviour, and support an improvement in service user quality of life *as well as* managing risk. • That an analysis of the strengths and needs of staff charged with implementing the plan have				

been taken into account in constructing the plan and any remedial actions undertaken.
- That an assessment of the goodness of fit of the plan with the resources and competencies of the staff group has been undertaken.
- That staff have been trained in implementing the plan using the three stage training model (verbal competence, role play competence, in vivo competence).

Stage 6. Ensure that all staff are trained in ethical approaches to reactive management

Key things to think about:	How we plan to do this?	By whom?	By when?	Date achieved
• Using the data from Stage 2, identify the typical scenarios that occur in the service that may require reactive management. • Ensuring that such strategies emphasise non-restrictive solutions wherever practicable. • Ensuring that training in physical interventions reflects the demands within the organisation (rather than training staff in a redundant series of interventions on the basis that they may be required at some point). • Ensuring that the training provider is BILD accredited and selected according to the criteria in section 11 of the Code of Practice (BILD, 2010).				

Stage 7. Identify proactive and reactive strategies for managing stress

Key things to think about:	How we plan to do this?	By whom?	By when?	Date achieved
• Developing systems for helping staff manage stress before it reaches unhelpful levels (eg, using mindfulness approaches, relation training, support groups, etc). • Having a robust system in place for supporting service users and staff in the aftermath of incidents where restrictive strategies have had to be employed. • Ensuring that organisational learning takes place following each incident and feeds back into the project plan.				

Stage 8. Establish a quality assurance system for monitoring service inputs and outputs

Key things to think about:	How we plan to do this?	By whom?	By when?	Date achieved
Employing a system such as Periodic Service Review to ensure that: • Actions around individual service user plans are correctly implemented on a routine basis. • That outcomes sought from these plans (in terms of improving quality of life and reducing behavioural challenges) are achieved. • Organisational actions around the reduction plan are being achieved. • Targets for reducing the use of restrictive practices are being achieved. • Remedial actions are set when this is not the case with any of the above.				

Stage 9. Celebrate success and take remedial action where necessary

Key things to think about:	How we plan to do this?	By whom?	By when?	Date achieved
Using the data from Stage 2 to: • Regularly publicise positive results (for example, in staff newsletters and in communications with stakeholder agencies). • Use the data to identify hot spots (that is, areas where reduction is not being achieved or where patterns begin to escalate) and determine what remedial action needs to take place.				

Summary

In this section, an attempt has been made to capture the good practice points about effective reduction strategies, PBS and good project management in a single template that will allow organisations to produce a bespoke plan for reducing their use of restraint, seclusion and emergency medication. The template should be regarded as a starting point and can be freely adapted to best suit the needs of the organisation using it; however, the author and publishers would be grateful if this source could always be credited when doing so.

6. Looking forward

This book has aimed to bring together a number of different ideas into a single publication whose central purpose is to help reduce the levels of use of restrictive practices currently seen in the UK and elsewhere.

Whether it can or not is an empirical question that can only be answered over time. Services that do embrace the principles and methodologies described here will, by virtue of adopting a data-driven approach, be in a position to contribute to the literature in this area. The newly founded *International Journal of Positive Behavioural Support* will certainly be interested in publishing such accounts.

More importantly, services which are successful in reducing restrictive strategy use will be able to demonstrate this to their users and purchasers; commissioners should also require that such data are made available when allocating contracts and this would be a significant help in differentiating between those who are only capable of talking the talk and those who can actually walk the walk.

If existing reports on effective restrictive practice reduction are correct and the analysis contained in this book accurate, then more systemic application of the identified strategies may in time impact on the rates of restraint, seclusion and emergency medication use reported in national surveys and described at the outset. While this may seem a grandiose ambition, in theory, it is perfectly achievable.

Now that would indeed be something to celebrate!

David Allen
February 2011

References

Adams, D and Allen, D (2001) Assessing the need for reactive behaviour management strategies in children with learning disabilities and severe challenging behaviour. *Journal of Intellectual Disability Research*, 45, 4, 335–343.

Albin, R W, Lucyshyn, J M, Horner, R H and Flannery, K B (1996) Contextual Fit for Behaviour Support Plans. A Model for "Goodness of Fit". In Koegel, L K, Koegel, R L and Dunlap, G (Eds) *Positive Behavioural Support. Including People with Difficult Behaviour in the Community*. Baltimore: Paul H. Brookes.

Allen, D (1999) Mediator Analysis: an overview of recent research on carers supporting people with intellectual disability and challenging behaviour. *Journal of Intellectual Disability Research*, 43, 4, 325–340.

Allen, D (2001) *Training Carers in Physical Interventions: Research Towards Evidence-Based Practice.* Kidderminster: BILD Publications.

Allen, D (2008) Risk and Prone Restraint-Reviewing the Evidence. In Nunno, M, Day, D and Bullard, L (Eds) *Examining the safety of high-risk interventions for children and young people.* New York: Child Welfare League of America.

Allen, D, Lowe, K, Brophy, S and Moore, K (2009) Predictors of Reactive Strategy Use in People with Challenging Behaviour. *Journal of Applied Research in Intellectual Disabilities*, 22, 159–168.

Allen, D, McDonald, L, Dunn, C and Doyle, A (1997) Changing care staff approaches to the prevention and management of aggression in a residential treatment unit for persons with mental retardation and challenging behaviour. *Research in Developmental Disabilities*, 18, 101–12.

Allen, D, Hawkins, S and Cooper, V (2006) Parents' use of physical interventions in the management of their children's challenging behaviour. *Journal of Applied Research in Intellectual Disabilities*, 19, 356–63.

Aman, M G, Singh, N N, Stewart, A W and Field, C J (1985) The Aberrant Behaviour Checklist: a behaviour rating scale for the assessment of treatment effects. *American Journal of Mental Retardation*, 89, 485–491.

Axlerod, S (1990) Myths that (mis) guide our profession. In: Repp, A C and Singh, N N (Eds) *Perspectives on the Use of Nonaversive and Aversive Interventions for Persons with Developmental Disabilities*. Sycamore: Sycamore, Il.

Baker, J A, Lovell, K and Harris, N (2007) Mental health professionals' psychotropic pro re nata (p.r.n) medication practices in acute inpatient mental health care: a qualitative study. *General Hospital Psychiatry*, 29, 163–168.

Baker, J A, Lovell, K and Harris, N (2008) The impact of a good practice manual on professional practice associated with psychotropic PRN in acute mental health wards: An exploratory study. *International Journal of Nursing Studies*, 45, 1403–1410.

Bambara, L M, Dunlap, G and Schwartz, I S (Eds) (2004) *Positive Behavioural Support: Critical Articles on Improving Practice for Individuals with Severe Disabilities*. Austin, Tx: Pro.ed.

Beadle-Brown, J, Hutchinson, A and Whelton, B (2009) A better life: the implementation and effect of person-centred active support in the Avenues Trust. *Tizard Learning Disability Review*, 13, 4, 15–24.

BILD (2008) *Easy Guide to Being Held Safely*. Second Edition. Kidderminster: BILD Publications.

BILD (2010) *Code of Practice for the Use of Physical Interventions. A guide for trainers and commissioners of training*. Third Edition. Kidderminster: BILD Publications.

Bisconer, S W, Zhang, X and Sine, L (1995) Impact of psychotropic medication and physical restraint review process on adults with mental retardation, psychiatric diagnoses and challenging behaviours. *Journal of Developmental and Physical Disabilities*, 7, 2, 123–135.

Bowie, V (1996) *Coping with Violence. A Guide for the Human Services*. Second Edition. London: Whiting and Birch.

Bullard, L, Fulmore, D and Johnson, K (2003) *Reducing the Use of Restraint and Seclusion. Promising Practices and Successful Strategies*. Washington: CWLA Press.

Campbell, J (2003) Efficacy of behavioural interventions for reducing problem behaviour in persons with autism: a quantitative synthesis of single-subject research. *Research in Developmental Disabilities*, 24, 120–138.

Child Welfare League of America (2004) *CWLA Best Practice Guidelines*. Washington DC: CWLA.

Carr, E G, Horner, R H, Turnbull, A P, Marquis, J G, McLaughlin, D M, McAtee, M L, Smith, C E, Ryan, K A, Ruef, M B and Doolabbh, A (1999) *Positive Behaviour Support for People with Developmental Disabilities: A Research Synthesis*. Washington: AAMR.

Carr, E G, Levin, L, McConnachie, G, Carlson, J I, Kemp, D C and Smith, CE (1994) *Communication-Based Intervention for Problem Behaviour. A User's Guide for Producing Positive Change*. Baltimore: Paul H. Brookes.

Colton, D (2004) *Checklist for assessing your organization's readiness for reducing seclusion and restraint*. Staunton, VA: Commonwealth Center for Children and Adolescence.

Colton, D (2008) Leadership's and Program's Role in Organizational and Cultural Change to Reduce Seclusion and Restraints. In Nunno, M, Day, D. and Bullard, L. (Eds) *Examining the safety of high-risk interventions for children and young people*. New York: Child Welfare League of America.

Crosland, K A, Cigales, M, Dunlap, G, Neff, B, Clark, H B, Giddings, T and Blanco, A (2008) Using staff training to decrease the use of restrictive procedures at two facilities for foster care children. *Research on Social Work Practice*, 18, 5, 401–409.

Dagnan, D and Weston, C (2006) Physical intervention with people with intellectual disabilities: The influence of cognitive and emotional variables. *Journal of Applied Research in Intellectual Disabilities*, 19, 219–22.

Dean, A J, Scott, J and McDermott, B M (2009) Changing utilization of pro re nata ('as needed') sedation in a child and adolescent psychiatric inpatient unit. *Australian and New Zealand Journal of Psychiatry*, 43, 360–365.

Deb, S, Kwok, H, Bertelli, M, Salvador-Carulla, L Bradley, E, Toor, J, and Barnhill, J (2009) International guide to prescribing psychotropic medication for the management of problem behaviours in adults with intellectual disabilities. *World Psychiatry*, 8, 181–186.

Delaney, K D (2006) Evidence base for practice: Reduction of restraint and seclusion use during child and adolescent psychiatric inpatient treatment. *Worldviews on Evidence-Based Nursing*, 3, 1, 19–30.

Department of Human Services (2009) *Physical restraint in disability services*. Melbourne: Office of the Senior Practitioner.

Deveau, R and McGill, P (2009) Physical interventions for adults with intellectual disabilities: Survey of use, policy, training and monitoring. *Journal of Applied Research in Intellectual Disabilities*, 22, 152–158.

Didden, R, Duker, P C and Korzilius, H (1997) Meta-analytic study on treatment effectiveness for problem behaviours in individuals who have mental retardation. *American Journal on Mental Deficiency*, 101, 387–399.

Didden, R, Korzilius, H, van Oorsouw, W and Sturmey, P (2006) Behavioural treatment of challenging behaviours in individuals with mild mental retardation: Meta-analysis of single-subject research. *American Journal on Mental Retardation*, 111, 4, 290–298.

Donat, D C (2002) Employing behavioural method to improve the context if care in a public psychiatric hospital: reducing hospital reliance on seclusion/restraint and psychotropic PRN medication. *Cognitive and Behavioural Practice*, 9, 28–37.

Donat, D C (2005) Encouraging alternatives to seclusion, restraint, and reliance on PRN drugs in a public psychiatric hospital. *Psychiatric Services*, 56, 9, 1105–1108.

Donnellan, A M and LaVigna, G W (1990) Myths about punishment. In: Repp, A C and Singh, N N (Eds) *Perspectives on the Use of Nonaversive and Aversive Interventions for Persons with Developmental Disabilities*. Sycamore Il: Sycamore.

Donnellan, A, LaVigna, G W, Negri-Scoultz, N, and Fassbender, L L (1998) *Progress without Punishment. Effective approaches for learners with behaviour problems.* New York: Teachers College Press.

Durand, V M (1990) *Severe Behaviour Problems. A Functional Communication Training Approach*. New York: Guilford Press.

Elford, H, Beail, N and Clarke, Z (2010) A Very Fine Line: Parents' Experiences of Using Restraint with Their Adult Son/Daughter with Intellectual Disabilities. *Journal of Applied Research in Intellectual Disabilities*, 23, 1, 75–84.

Emerson, E (2002) The prevalence of use of reactive management strategies in community-based services in the UK. In Allen, D (Ed) *Ethical Approaches to physical interventions to physical interventions. Responding to challenging behaviour in people with intellectual disabilities*. Kidderminster: BILD Publications.

Emerson, E and McGill, P (1989) Normalization and Applied Behaviour Analysis: Values and Technology in Services for People with Learning Difficulties. *Behavioural Psychotherapy*, 17, 101–117.

Evans, D, Wood, J and Lambert, L (2003) Patient injury and physical restraint devices: a systematic review. *Journal of Advanced Nursing*, 41, 3, 274–282.

Feldman, M A, Atkinson, L, Foti-Gervais, L and Condillac, R (2004) Formal versus informal interventions for challenging behaviours in persons with intellectual disabilities. *Journal of Intellectual Disability Research*, 48, 60–8.

Foxx, R M (2005) Severe aggressive and self-destructive behaviour: The myth of nonaversive treatment of severe behaviour. In: Jacobsen, J W, Foxx, R M and Mulick, J A (Eds) *Controversial Therapies for Developmental Disabilities. Fad, Fashion, and Science in Professional Practice*. Routledge: New York.

Gaskin, C J, Elsom, S J and Happell, B (2007) Interventions for reducing seclusion in psychiatric facilities. *British Journal of Psychiatry*, 191, 298–303.

Guess, D, Helmstetter, E, Turnbull, H R and Knowlton, S (1987) *Use of Aversive Procedures with Persons who are Disabled: An Historical Review and Critical Analysis*. Seattle: Association for Persons with Severe Handicaps.

Harvey, S T, Boaer, D Meyer, L M and Evans, I M (2009) Updating a meta-analysis of intervention research with challenging behaviour: Treatment validity and standards of practice. *Journal of Intellectual & Developmental Disability*, 34, 1, 67–80.

Harris, J, Allen, D, Cornick, M Jefferson, A and Mills, R (1996) *Physical Interventions. A Policy Framework*. Kidderminster: BILD Publications.

Harris, J, Cornick, M Jefferson, A and Mills, R (2008) *Physical Interventions. A Policy Framework. Second Edition*. Kidderminster: BILD Publications.

Hilton, M F and Whitefoot, H A (2008) Pro re nata medication for psychiatric inpatients: time to act. *Australian and New Zealand Journal of Psychiatry*, 42, 555–564.

Hsen-Hsing Ma (2009) The effectiveness of intervention on the behaviour of individuals with autism. *Behaviour Modification*, 33, 3, 339–359.

Huckshorn, K A (2004) Reducing seclusion and restraint use in mental health settings. Core strategies for prevention. *Journal of Psychosocial Nursing*, 42, 9, 22–33.

Huckshorn, K A (2005) *Six Core Strategies to Reduce the Use of Seclusion and Restraint Planning Tool*. Alexandia, VA: National Technical Assistance Centre.

Jefferson, A (2009) Reflections on Accreditation. In Allen, D (Ed) *Ethical Approaches to Physical Intervention. Volume II. Closing the Agenda*. Kidderminster: BILD Publications.

Jones, E, Perry, J, Lowe, K, Felce, D, Toogood, S, Dunstan, F, Allen, D and Pagler, J (1999) Opportunity and the promotion of activity among adults with severe intellectual disability living in community residences: the impact of training staff in active support. *Journal of Intellectual Disability Research*, 43, 3, 164–178.

LaVigna, G W and Willis, T (2003) Counter-intuitive strategies for crisis management within anon-aversive framework. In Allen, D (Ed) *Ethical Approaches to physical interventions to physical interventions. Responding to challenging behaviour in people with intellectual disabilities*. Kidderminster: BILD Publications.

LaVigna, G W, Willis, T J, Shaull, J F, Abedi, M and Sweitzer, E (1994) *The Periodic Service Review. A total quality assurance system for human services and education*. Maryland: Paul H. Brookes.

Leggett, J and Silvester, J (2003) Care staff attributions for violent incidents involving male and female patients: A field study. *British Journal of Clinical Psychology*, 42, 393–406.

Lowe, K, Allen, D, Brophy, S and Moore, K (2005) The Management and Treatment of Challenging Behaviours. *Tizard Learning Disability Review*, 10, 34–7.

Linscheid, T R and Landau, R J (1993) Going "all out" pharmacologically? A re-examination of Berkman & Meyer's "Alternative strategies and multiple outcomes in remediation of severe self-injury: Going 'all out' nonaversively." *Mental Retardation*, 31, 1, 1–6.

Lucyshen, J M, Dunlap, G and Albin, R W (Eds) (2002) *Families & Positive Behaviour Support. Addressing Problem Behaviour in Family Contexts*. Baltimore: Paul H. Brookes.

Luiselli, J K (2009) Physical Restraint of People with Intellectual Disability: A Review of Implementation Reduction and Elimination Procedures. *Journal of Applied Research in Intellectual Disabilities*, 22, 2,126–134.

Kennedy, C H and Meyer, K A (1998) The use of psychotropic medication for people with severe disabilities and challenging behaviour: Current status and future directions. *Journal of the Association for Persons with Severe Handicaps*, 23, 2, 83–97.

Koegel, L K, Koegel, R L and Dunlap, G (Eds) (1996) *Positive Behavioural Support. Including People with Difficult Behaviour in the Community*. Baltimore: Paul H. Brookes.

Marquis, J G Horner, R H, Carr, E G, Turnbull, A P, Thompson, M, Behrens, G A, Magito-McLaughlin, D, McAtee, M L, Smith, C E, Ryan, K A and Doolabh, A (2000) A meta-analysis of positive behaviour support. In Gersten, R, Schiller, E P and Vaughn, S (Eds) *Contemporary Special Education Research*. New York: Lawrence Erlbaum Associates.

Marshall, T (2004) Audit of the use of psychotropic medication for challenging behaviour in a community learning disability service. *Psychiatric Bulletin*, 28, 447–450.

Martin, A, Krieg, H, Esposito, F, Stubbe, D and Cardona, L (2008) Reduction of restraint and seclusion through collaborative problem solving: a five-year prospective inpatient study. *Psychiatric Services*, 59, 12, 1406–1412.

Mason, T (1996) Seclusion and learning disabilities: Research and deduction. *British Journal of Developmental Disabilities*, 17, 149–59.

Masters, K J (2008) Modernizing Seclusion and Restraint. In Nunno, M, Day, D and Bullard, L (Eds) *Examining the safety of high-risk interventions for children and young people.* New York: Child Welfare League of America.

Matson, J L (1995) *Diagnostic Assessment for the Severely Handicapped-II (DASH-II).* Disability Consultants LLC: Baton Rouge.

Matson, J L and Neal, D (2009) Psychotropic medication use for challenging behaviours in persons with intellectual disabilities: An overview. *Research in Developmental Disabilities*, 30, 572–586.

McBrien, J and Felce, D (1992) *Working with People who Have Severe Learning Difficulty and Challenging Behaviour. A Practical Handbook on the Behavioural Approach.* Kidderminster: British Institute of Mental Handicap.

McDonnell, A (2009) The effectiveness of training in physical intervention. In: Allen, D (Ed) *Ethical approaches to physical interventions. Volume 2.* Kidderminster: BILD Publications.

McGill, P, Murphy, G and Kelly-Pike, A (2009) Frequency of use and characteristics of people with intellectual disabilities subject to physical interventions. *Journal of Applied Research in Intellectual Disabilities*, 22, 152–158.

Meyer, L H and Berkman, K A (1993) What's straw and what's real? A reply to Linscheid and Landau. *Mental Retardation*, 31, 7–14.

Meyer, L and Evans, I M (1989) *Nonaversive intervention for behaviour problems. A manual for home and community.* Baltimore: Paul H. Brookes.

Mental Health Act Commission (2006) *In Place of Fear? Eleventh Biennial Report.* London: TSO.

Mulick, J A and Butter, E M (2005) Positive behaviour support: a paternalistic utopian delusion. In: Jacobsen, J W, Foxx, R M and Mulick, J A (Eds) *Controversial Therapies for Developmental Disabilities.*

Fad, Fashion, and Science in Professional Practice. Routledge: New York.

Muralidharan, S and Fenton, S (2006) *Containment strategies for people with serious mental illness*. The Cochrane Database of Systematic Reviews 3, 1–10

National Institute for Clinical Excellence (NICE) (2005) *Violence. The short-term management of disturbed/violent behaviour in in-patient psychiatric settings and emergency departments*. London: Royal College of Nursing.

Nelstrop, L, Chandler-Oatts, J, Bingley, W, Bleetman, T, Corr, F, Cronin-Davis. J, Fraher, D, Jones, S, Gournay, K, Johnston, S, Pereira, S, Pratt, P, Tucker, R and Tsuchiya, A (2006) A systemic review of the safety and effectiveness of restraint and seclusion as interventions for the short-term management of violence in adult psychiatric inpatient settings and emergency departments. *Worldviews on Evidence-Based Nursing*, 3, 1, 8–18.

Noone, S J and Hastings, R P (2009) Building psychological resilience in support staff caring for people with intellectual disabilities. Pilot evaluation of an acceptance-based intervention. *Journal of Intellectual Disabilities*, 13, 1, 43–53.

O'Neill, R E, Horner, R H, Albin, R W, Sprague, J R, Storey, K and Newton, J S (1997) *Functional Assessment and Program development for Problem Behaviour. A Practical Handbook*. Pacific Grove, CA: Brooks/Cole.

Paley, S (2009) BILD Factsheet: Time out and seclusion. Available from *www.bild.org.uk/docs/05faqs/Time_Out_Seclusion_09.pdf*

Paterson, B, Leadbetter, D, Miller, G and Crichton, J (2008) Adopting a public health model to reduce violence and restraints in children's residential facilities. In Nunno, M, Day, D and Bullard, L (Eds) *Examining the safety of high-risk interventions for children and young people*. New York: Child Welfare League of America.

Paton, C, Barnes, T, Cavanagh, M, Taylor, D and Lelliot, P (2008) High-dose and combination antipsychotic prescribing in acute adult wards in the UK: the challenges posed by p.r.n prescribing. *British Journal of Psychiatry*, 192, 435–439.

Patrick, V, Schleifer, S J, Nurenberg, J R and Gill, K J (2006) An initiative to curtail the use of antipsychotic polypharmacy in a state hospital. *Psychiatric Services*, 57, 1, 21–23.

Rangecroft, M E H, Tyrer, S P and Berney, T P (1997) The use of seclusion and emergency medication in a hospital for people for people with learning disability. *British Journal of Psychiatry*, 170, 273–7.

Robertson, J, Emerson, E, Pinkney, L, Caeser, E, Felce, D, Meek, A, Carr, D, Lowe, K, Knapp, M and Hallam, A (2005) Treatment and management of challenging behaviours in congregate and non-congregate community-based supported accommodation. *Journal of Intellectual Disability Research*, 49, 63–72.

Rowland, G and Treece, S (2000) Violent incidents and the use of antipsychotic medication within a specialist challenging behaviour unit: an evaluation of the Poole approach to challenging behaviour. *British Journal of Learning Disabilities*, 28, 91–101.

Ryan, J B, Peterson, R L, Tetreault, G and van der Hagen, E (2008) Reducing the use of seclusion and restraint in day school program. In Nunno, M, Day, D and Bullard, L (Eds) *Examining the safety of high-risk interventions for children and young people.* New York: Child Welfare League of America.

Sailas, E and Fenton, M (2000) *Seclusion and restraint for people with serious mental illness. The Cochrane Database of Systematic Reviews,* Issue 1

Sanders, K (2009) The effects of an action plan, staff training, management support and monitoring on restraint use and costs of work related injuries. *Journal of Applied Research in Intellectual Disabilities*, 22, 216–22.

Scotti, J R, Evans, I M, Meyer, L M and Walker, P (1991) A meta-analysis of intervention research with problem behaviour: Treatment validity and standards of practice. *Journal of Intellectual Disability Research*, 96, 233–256.

Singh, N N and Winton, A S W (1984) Behavioural monitoring of pharmacological interventions for self-injury. *Applied Research in Mental Retardation*, 5, 161–170.

Singh, N N, Lancioini, G E, Winton, A S W, Curtis, W J, Wahler, R G, Sabaawi, M, Singh, J and McAleavey, K (2006) Mindful staff increase learning and reduce aggression in adults with developmental disabilities. *Research in Developmental Disabilities*, 27, 345–58.

Singh, N N, Lancioini, G E, Winton, A S W, Singh, A S, Askins, A D and Singh, J (2009) Mindful staff can reduce the use of physical restraints when providing care to individuals with intellectual disabilities. *Journal of Applied Research in Intellectual Disabilities*, 22, 194–202.

Smith, G S, Davis, R H, Bixler, E O, Lin, H, Altenor, A, Altenor, R, Hardentstine, B S and Kopchick, MS (2005) Pennsylvania State Hospital System's Seclusion and Restraint Reduction Plan. *Psychiatric Services*, 56, 9, 1115–1122.

Spirrison, C L and Grosskopf, L G (1991) Psychotropic medication efficacy graphs: An application of applied behaviour analysis. *Mental Retardation*, 3, 139–147.

Sturmey, P (1999) Correlates of restraint use in an institutional population. *Research in Developmental Disabilities*, 20, 339–46.

Sturmey, P (2009) Restraint, seclusion and PRN medication in English services for people with learning disabilities administered by the National Health Service: An analysis of the 2007 National Audit Survey. *Journal of Applied Research in Intellectual Disabilities*, 22, 140–144.

Sturmey, P and McGlyn, A P (2002) Restraint reduction. In Allen, D (Ed) *Responding to Challenging Behaviour in Persons with Intellectual*

Disabilities: Ethical approaches to physical intervention. Kidderminster: BILD Publications.

Sturmey, P, Lott, J D, Laud, R and Matson, J L (2005) Correlates of restraint use in an institutionalized population: A replication. *Journal of Intellectual Disability Research*, 49, 501–6.

Toogood, S, Drury, G, Gilsenan, K, Parry, D, Roberts, K and Sheriff, S (2009) Establishing a context to reduce challenging behaviour using procedures from active support: a clinical case example. *Tizard Learning Disability Review*, 14, 4, 29–36.

Thomas, B, Jones, M, Johns, P and Trauer, T (2006) P.r.n. medication use in a psychiatric high-dependency unit following the introduction of a nurse-led activity programme. *International Journal of Mental Health Nursing*, 15, 266–271.

Thompson, R W, Huefner, J C, Vollmer, D G Daviis, J L and Daly, D L (2008) A case study of organisational intervention to reduce physical interventions: Creating, effective, harm-free environments. In Nunno, M, Day, D and Bullard, L (Eds) *Examining the safety of high-risk interventions for children and young people.* New York: Child Welfare League of America.

Tyrer, P, Oliver-Africano, P, Ahmed, Z, Bouras, B, Cooray, S, Deb, S, Murphy, D, Hare, M, Meade, M, Reece. B, Kramo, K, Bhaumik, S, Harley, D, Regan, A, Thomas, D, Rao, B, North, B, Eliahoo, J, Karatela, S, Soni, A and Crawford, M (2008) Risperidone, haloperidol, and placebo in the treatment of aggressive challenging behaviour in patients with intellectual disability: a randomised controlled trial. *The Lancet*, 371, 9606, 57–63.

Unwin, G I and Deb, S (2010) The use of medication to manage behaviour problems in adults with intellectual disability: a national guideline. *Advances in Mental Health and Intellectual Disabilities*, 4, 3, 4–11.

Whicher, E, Morrison, M and Douglass-Hall, P (2002) *'As required'* *medication regimes for seriously mentally ill people in hospital.* The Cochrane Database for Systematic Reviews, 1.

Whittaker, S (1993) The reduction of aggression in people with learning difficulties: A review of psychological methods. *British Journal of Clinical Psychology*, 32, 1–37.

Williams, D E (2010) Reducing and eliminating restraint of people with developmental disabilities and severe behaviour disorders: An overview of recent research. *Research in Developmental Disabilities*, 31, 1142–1148.

Zarkowska, E and Clements, J (1996) *Problem Behaviour and People with Severe Disabilities. The STAR Approach.* London: Chapman & Hall.